LAST LAUGHS

COMPILED BY GRAHAM AND SYLVANA NOWN

CARTOONS BY ALBERT

WARD LOCK LIMITED · LONDON

First published in Great Britain in 1984
by Ward Lock Limited, 82 Gower Street,
London WC1E 6EQ, a Pentos Company.

Text set in 11/13 Palatino
by Fakenham Photosetting Limited,
Fakenham, Norfolk.

Printed and bound in Portugal by Gris Impressores S.A.R.L.

D.L. 5340/84

British Library Cataloguing in Publication Data

Nown, Graham
   Last laughs.
   1. Death–Anecdotes, factial, satire, etc.
   I. Title   II. Nown, Sylvana
   306.9'0207   HQ1073

   ISBN 0–7063–6292–6

A selection of skeletal tales from the vaults of
the Oddfax Collection–Graham and Sylvana
Nown's library of almost a million newspaper
cuttings devoted to the bizarre and unusual.
The collection, covering 47,000 subjects, dates
back to 1800.

Thanks to the splendid death-watchers of the newspapers
and magazines quoted–and their permission to use material.
If there are any we have overlooked, or failed to nail down,
grave apologies.

Contents

Foreword

When it comes to Death, you really can't be too careful. It has the nastiest habit of polishing us off before we have time to, well, compose ourselves.

Poor Col. Roscoe Tatem of the US Army is a case in point. He was placed in charge of Independence Day celebrations in Richmond, Virginia. And, being obsessed with shining brass and boot polish, was anxious to make sure everything went right.

Each cannon taking part in the 21-gun salute had to be gleaming and loaded with just the right amount of powder and shot. Each fuse had to be cut to precisely the same length, to within one tenth of an inch.

Col. Tatem gave the order to light fuses. But he couldn't resist a final check to see if the guns were lined up properly. He took a brief step forward – and was blown to pieces.

Life's Col. Tatems climb out of their crypts throughout this book. It is a collection of press reports – all deadpan of course – about the strange incidents that spring from our preoccupation with Death.

We hope it may serve as a constant reminder that its taste is everywhere – or at least the Solinger family think so . . .

In the lean days after World War II the postman used to deliver food parcels to their German village from relatives in the United States.

4

Among the beans and butter in one delivery was a tin of appetizing-looking grey powder. When Frau Solinger added water and boiled it up, everyone agreed it was the best soup they had tasted in years.

The following day a letter arrived from America asking if they had safely received the remains of their granny. It had been her last request to be buried back on German soil.

Mind how you go . . .

Where There's a Will . . .

Unbottled at Last

The will of a Wall Street broker instructed:
'To my wife I leave her lover and the knowledge that I was not the fool she thought I was. To my son I leave the pleasure of earning a living. For thirty-five years he thought the pleasure was mine. He was mistaken.

'To my daughter I leave £20,000 – she will need it, for the only proper business her husband ever did was to marry her.

'To my valet I leave the clothes he has been stealing from me for the past ten years, and also the fur coat he wore last winter at Palm Beach.

'To my chauffeur I leave my cars. He almost ruined them and I want him to have the satisfaction of finishing the job.

'Lastly, to my partner, I leave the suggestion that he take some other man in with him if he ever expects to do any business.'

Titbits, 1948

The End of the Line

Bitter words were recently contained in the will of a prominent railway official.

'My estate,' he commented, 'would have been considerably larger if it had not been for my unfortunate marriage with the cleverest-known daylight robber. My associations with this perambulating vinegar cruet I consider to have cost me over £4000. I leave her the sum of one shilling.'

Ideas, 1925

A Brother's Last Laugh

Farm worker Guiseppe Camba quit his job in Naples, and started living it up after receiving a letter from an American lawyer.

It told him his long-lost brother, Carlo, had died in San Francisco leaving one million dollars and no other heir.

But then came another letter revealing his share of the fortune was just £8 – 'to buy a drink and reflect on your wickedness.'

It was Carlo's revenge on Guiseppe for pinching his fiancee forty years ago.

The Sun, 1980

The Last Post

A vengeful husband left his wife a farthing, with instructions that it should be sent to her by post in an unstamped envelope.

In making his bequest the testator knew that his widow would be charged eightpence for the delivery of an unstamped letter containing coin.

Ideas, 1925

Coughing up the Cash

Samuel Brett, of Philadelphia, did not like causing a fuss during his lifetime, so he left a parting shot in his will.

All his married life he resented the fact that his wife never allowed him to smoke cigars in the house.

He suffered in silence to keep the domestic peace.

When he died in 1960, however, he left a will bequeathing a fortune of one million dollars to his wife—on condition that she smoked, 'to the end', five cigars a day.

Titbits, 1962

Leg-Puller

Mr Collins, a Londoner, bequeathed his wife 'one pair of trousers free of duty and carriage paid, as a symbol of what she wanted to wear in my lifetime, but did not.'

Weekend, 1981

Sourpuss

Woodbury Rand, a Boston lawyer, penalized his relatives for casualness to cats. He had promised to leave them £4000 each, but after one of them tripped over the office cat and no one sympathized with puss, he cut them all out of his will.

Instead, he left £20,000 to the cat.

Answers, 1950

Revenge from the Grave

The four daughters-in-law of Mrs Jennifer Hayward, an American widow, had never got on with the old lady.

But she summoned them to her deathbed and gave each a splendid diamond ring.

However, when one of them tried to sell her ring she got a shock. 'It's glass,' the jeweller told her.

Mrs Hayward's maid, to whom she left her house in Atlanta, Georgia, said: 'She had a glass decanter stopper carefully cut to pay them back for their neglect of her.'

Weekend, 1982

Some Thought

Wealthy Austrian Rudolf Dieterburger promised his relatives that he would be thinking of them when he made his will.

He certainly did. He left them some of his thoughts.

To his nephew he left thoughts about the £78,000 he might have left him—but didn't. Other relatives got similar thoughts—because they had all neglected Rudolf in his old age. Nobody received cash.

Weekend, 1981

Getting Knotted

An Australian woman recently willed one shilling to her husband, to be spent on a rope to hang himself.

Answers, 1942

A vindictive testator in the Midlands not long ago bequeathed all his property to his daughter, on condition that she paid the sum of three and a half pence 'for the purchase of a hempen cord or halter for my dear wife, which I trust she will make use of without delay.'

Ideas, 1925

At the Braker's

A Mr Braker of Melbourne, Australia, stipulated in his will
that the proceeds from the sale of his expensive car were to
go to his former girlfriend.
  His wife, Mrs Jill Braker, sold the car for £5.

Weekend, 1980

For the Greater Good

A malicious testator, embittered by his conjugal experience,
recorded it thus in his will:
  'I have always declared that my wife was the dearest
woman in the world, and I am convinced that if anyone
should be rash enough to marry her, he will find her so.
  'To deter as far as possible anyone from making such a
ruinous experiment, I leave her nothing.'

Daily Chronicle, 1920

Shellshocked

A Bristol sailor recently left his wife one shilling 'to buy nuts,
as she seems to get more pleasure from sitting cracking
them, than from mending my stockings.'

Ideas, 1920

Thanks for the Memory

After a lifetime of unhappiness a husband has cut his wife
out of his will. He wrote: 'She has led me a hell-upon-earth
life and when it pleases the Almighty to call me, it will also
please me to be taken from such a dreadful woman.'

Titbits, 1950

Going Down for the Last Time

Hans Muller, a Munich miser, was persecuted by his
relatives throughout his life. They were curious to learn that
his will was to be read in a certain upstairs room.

They soon knew why when the floor collapsed. Cunning
old Hans had previously sawn through the joists.

Answers, 1953

French Leave

A doctor, Jean Berthier, of St Maude, France, bequeathed everything to his wife, saying: 'I do not know her present whereabouts, but she once did me the great favour of deserting me.

'I leave her everything, on condition she marries again. I want to make certain that at least one human being will be sorry I died.'

Weekend, 1982

Red Letter Day

In his will, Fred Eggerman, of Paterson, New Jersey, bequeathed the bulk of his 12,000-dollar estate to 'the first male child born July 2nd 1946 at Paterson General Hospital – the forty-fifth anniversary of my birth.'

The money was claimed by Robert Martin de Boer, of Wayne. Mr Eggerman's widow was left one dollar.

Grit, 1961

Getting the Chop

A Canadian disapproved all his life of his lazy nephew. The playboy was neatly punished in his uncle's will. He was to receive a legacy of £30,000 – on one condition. That he had to spend it all on firewood, and sell the wood himself.

Answers, 1953

A Woman Crossed

In East Ham churchyard a tombstone has been placed crossways. The woman interred is said to have been born cross, lived cross, married a Mr Cross and died cross.

Her dying request was to be buried cross, and this has now been carried out.

Cassell's Saturday Journal, 1898

Brief Despatches

Some unscheduled departures

Stringalonga Max

A Berlin thief, Max Kemperdick, was brought to summary justice by a string of stolen sausages.

He had broken into an apartment, filled his pockets with valuables, and finally snatched a string of sausages from the larder.

As he was escaping through the kitchen window, the sausages caught on a nail and hanged him.

Reveille, 1954

What a Blow

While knocking a perambulator spring with a hammer, Mrs Ruth Evans, aged 43, of Billington, Bedfordshire, was struck on the head by the hammer rebounding and was killed by her own blow.

The Star, 1923

The Great Divide

Paris, Saturday. While a farmer, Monsieur Bousquet, was superintending operations at a sawmill, near Riberac, where some of his trees were being converted into planks, a cow tethered in the yard caught its foot in its chain.

M. Bousquet stooped to free the animal which, however, butted him violently. He was tossed a distance of 9 ft, where he fell beneath the circular saw. Before the saw could be stopped he was cut completely in two.

Sunday Observer, 1925

Shocking

The morbidly sensitive can be driven into a paroxysm of fright by the slightest alarms.

The famous French Marshal de Monterval, an extremely superstitious man, died at a public dinner from fright caused by a salt cellar being upset in his lap.

Frederick I of Prussia died from fright caused by the spectacle of his mad wife, who had escaped from her keepers, suddenly appearing before him, covered with blood from a self-inflicted wound.

Answers, 1891

A Crashing Bore

A distressing accident at a funeral was reported. The floor collapsed at the home of the deceased, in Birmingham, and nine mourners fell through into the cellar.

Yorkshire Evening Press, 1893

Soap

An old man who had refused to wash for seventeen years fell foul of the sanitation authorities in Oaxaca City, Mexico, who forced him to take a bath. He died of shock.

Titbits, 1938

Wheels Up

Willie Rolls, the famous roller-skating actor, who has played the music halls for thirty years, fell dead in a Detroit theatre.

The audience was so enthusiastic over his skating performance that they called him three times to repeat his show. Even then they were not satisfied, and insisted on a fourth encore.

The curtain was rising once more when Rolls collapsed from exertion.

Daily Express, 1924

Drowning Glory

Baptism candidate John Blue, 47, drowned when he lost his footing during a total immersion ceremony in a lake near Boston, America. The pastor–like bachelor Blue a non-swimmer–said: 'Maybe God wanted him.'

Evening Standard, 1983

Don't Look Back

Charles Joiner, 68, was so superstitious that he would not turn round on the stairs.

But his superstition killed him as he walked backwards downstairs at his home to investigate a noise.

He fell backwards, fracturing his thigh, and died at hospital.

Daily Herald, 1962

The Man who Popped Off

Having placed an electric light bulb in his armchair, Mr Andrew Berry, aged 77, of Southend Road, Wickford, Essex, forgot it and sat on it.

The bulb exploded with a loud report. Mr Berry was badly cut and died in Southend Hospital on Saturday.

Daily Mail, 1930

Biting Back

Manslaughter by animals

Gunned Down by a Moth

After giving a dinner party the Princess Caravella of Naples
went to lie down in order to refresh herself for a dance, and
was later found shot through the heart.

Suspicion pointed to her husband, who was known to be
of a jealous disposition, and he was arrested.

But a moth had killed the famous Neapolitan beauty.
Lured by the light of the princess's bed lamp, it had fluttered
against it, singed its wings and fallen onto the loaded gun the
princess always kept beside her bed. In its death agonies it
released the hair spring of the weapon.

Titbits, 1926

Speared by a Bull

At a bullfight in Corunna a few days ago the matador was
about to kill the bull, when the beast twisted round and
flung up its head.

It caught the sword between its horns, and sent it spinning
into the air. Flying like a javelin, it struck a spectator in the
breast. He died on the way to hospital.

Answers, 1934

Stabbed by a Mule

A Kansas farmer was killed by the mule he was clipping for
hot weather. The mule kicked the shears out of his hand.
Their sharp point pierced an artery in his arm, and he bled to
death before aid could reach him.

Reveille, 1954

Shot by a Fish

The tragic death has been reported of a Canadian fisherman, shot by the fish he had just caught.

The fish, plopping in the bottom of the canoe, got tangled in a fishing line which fouled itself round the trigger of a loaded rifle. The gun went off and the fisherman was killed.

Pearson's Weekly, 1931

Drowned by a Pike

Nothing could be more relaxing than a sunny afternoon spent by the riverside fishing. Yet this peaceful hobby brought death to a Monsieur Buron, of Luneville, France, only a few days ago.

M. Buron had been lucky enough to hook a pike. The pike put up a struggle and pulled its captor into the river. There, Buron's head hit a stone. He was stunned and drowned.

Reveille, 1954

Grand Finales

Some unusual human rites

One Leg in the Grave

Frank Molina had one foot in the grave yesterday. His left
one.

Four days ago Frank, 71, had his left leg amputated in a
Madrid clinic.

And yesterday, upset that it was going to rest all by itself,
he had it buried in the cemetery with full funeral honours.

Frank, who had the operation after a thrombosis, was not
well enough to attend the ceremony.

But he said: 'As soon as I leave hospital I shall buy some
flowers, hire a taxi and go and put them on the tomb of my
leg.'

Frank, who paid £20 for a wooden casket, added: 'That leg
was part of me. I wouldn't feel right if it wasn't buried
properly.'

Daily Mirror, 1982

The Tobacco King's Last Drag

Requests by persons on the verge of death can put their children under great obligations.

An Austrian tobacco king, before he died recently, vowed that his son, who was to inherit his large fortune, should dress as a girl until he was 14 years of age.

Dorset Daily Echo, 1934

Going Cheap

A church raffle was scrapped after parishioners protested that one of the prizes–a free funeral–was in bad taste.

It was one of seven prizes in a draw organized to help raise £500 for parish church funds at Feckenham, Hereford and Worcester.

Daily Express, 1982

Last Word

American pastor James Dotson who died last Tuesday, aged 27, yesterday delivered the sermon at his own funeral at Mansfield, Ohio–on videotape.

The Sun, 1982

Wife's Last Laugh

Joker Harold Harris was late for his own funeral–on his wife Janet's orders.

Harold, 66, had always kept her waiting when they went out. So she told pall-bearers to pause for a minute before entering the church with his coffin.

She said: 'Harold never took life seriously and would have appreciated it.'

Harold, of Duns Tew, Oxfordshire, had ordered a bottle of Guinness and his favourite pipe to be buried with him.

Daily Star, 1982

Not to be Sneezed At

Whimsical indeed was the will of Mistress Meg Thompson, of Boyle Street, Burlington Gardens. Her passion was Scotch snuff.

Her will said that as she had never found any flowers as refreshing and fragrant as the 'precious powder', her servant was to take care that her body was covered with the best Scotch snuff.

Six men, the greatest snuff takers in the parish, were to carry her to the grave, each wearing a snuff-coloured beaver hat instead of mourning.

Six old maids of like snuff-taking character were to act as pallbearers. They were to be supplied with boxes of snuff wherewith to refresh themselves on the road.

Twenty pounds was paid to the servant, on condition that she walked before the corpse distributing 'every twenty yards a large handful of Scotch snuff to the ground and upon the crowd.'

Titbits, 1889

The Final Score

The ashes of centre-forward Sid Trickett, who scored eight goals with his head at Torrington football ground in 1948, found a final resting place beneath the goal that was the scene of his greatest triumph.

Daily Mail, 1983

Holy Smoke

A country cemetery funeral in Georgia had a tragically bizarre twist—just as the preacher said, 'We never know who is going next,' a bolt of lightning killed one of the mourners.

Witnesses were stunned by what they described as being 'like a ball of fire out of the sky.'

The grandson of the woman who was being buried was killed, his wife was knocked unconscious and the lightning also struck a grave-digger.

Weekly News, 1982

A Grave Omission

The funeral service had started, and the vicar had spoken the opening sentences when he announced that there was a technical hitch.

The Rev. John Brown slipped quietly out of church at St Mary's, Crich, Derbyshire, took off his coat, picked up a spade—and then started to dig the grave.

For owing to a misunderstanding the most important item in the funeral had been neglected.

He got the four bearers and the undertaker to help him. Working in relays they had the grave ready in twenty minutes.

The Dispatch, 1956

A Flash in the Pan

Capital punishment by electrocution has never been adopted in Abyssinia, despite King Merekek's purchase of an electric chair from America.

He overlooked the fact that his country had not a single power station. When he realized that murderers would have to be disposed of by other means, he decided to use the chair as a throne.

Weekly Telegraph, 1948

Brimming with Cheer

In his will, Mr Hayward Barber, a merchant of Keats Grove, Hampstead, who died in June, directed the executors to provide new hats for all his relatives and friends attending his funeral 'as a slight relief to the unpleasant ceremony.'

Daily Mirror, 1934

Mind How You Go

An unusual accident occurred during a funeral at Chalfont St Giles, Buckinghamshire, says a correspondent.

While the bearers were about to lower the coffin containing the body of an aged resident, one of them slipped on the wet boards and fell into the grave.

His fall caused the other bearers to lose their hold, and the coffin fell upon him, breaking two of his ribs.

The Star, 1925

Boxing Clever

After a resident of Lima, Peru, died, two rival undertakers, trying to get the business, came to blows at his door.

After a bitter fight, one was left unconscious and the other took to his heels. Meanwhile a third undertaker turned up with a coffin and got the job.

Weekend, 1964

A Tight Fit

Mourners were assembled round a grave at Edmonton Cemetery and the coffin was about to be lowered. It was then found that the grave was not wide enough.

The funeral party withdrew for about twenty minutes while the grave was widened. The facts were reported to Edmonton Council who have ordered an inquiry.

The deceased was an exceptionally stout woman.

Daily Mirror, 1924

Vanishing Act

The strange funeral service took place in a busy street. There was no body in the coffin. For the dead man lay at the bottom of a hole in the town's main street.

Planks had been laid across the top of the hole.

Over them relatives laid a huge wreath of chrysanthemums.

Two braziers flared by the edge of the giant hole. Their flames cast a yellow glow over the faces of the mourners.

The tragedy began early one dark morning when Thomas Holland strode through the Hanley district of Stoke-on-Trent on his way to work. Despite the rain he whistled and sang happily. Suddenly the singing stopped.

In the gloom a workman saw 56-year-old Thomas throw up his arms and disappear. The ground beneath him had given way and he lay at the foot of an old disused pit shaft.

His body was never recovered.

Weekend, 1983

A Matchless Send-off

Upon the request of a doctor who died recently, a pipe was placed in one hand, a box of matches in the other, while a tobacco pouch rested on his chest.

Dorset Daily Echo, 1934

A Cliffhanger Ending

An unusual coroner's inquest was held on the rim of Mount Kilauea, an active Hawaiian volcano.

A young man named Sylvester Nunes had shot his girlfriend Margaret Enos when she refused to marry him, and leapt with her body into the crater of Halemaumau, where Pele, the fire goddess, dwells.

The inquest jury, who had to climb to the summit of Kilaueu, were issued with binoculars to view the bodies, 1000 feet below at the very edge of the bubbling larva.

A funeral was proposed in which the minister would throw dynamite to bury them. Finally a Japanese contractor offered to recover the bodies by being lowered into the crater, suspended in a cage, for 1000 dollars.

The Literary Digest, 1932

The Last Waltz

Beside an open grave an orchestra sat playing a waltz. It was fulfilling the last wish of an elderly music lover who, on his death bed, had directed that he should be buried to the strains of *The Blue Danube*.

Reveille, 1954

Travelling Light

One of the most astonishing mistakes ever made at a burial occurred on Monday afternoon at Shooter's Hill Cemetery, when a flower-bedecked coffin was lowered into a grave with solemn funeral rites, while all the time the body was lying in the undertaker's shed.

The body was that of Police Constable George Parker, who met with a fatal accident on his allotment.

The body was taken to the undertaker's offices in a shell, ready for placing in a coffin by two workmen. Instead of doing this they screwed the coffin down and placed it in the hearse.

The funeral cortège passed slowly to the cemetery, being met at the gates by 100 of the dead constable's comrades, two divisional inspectors and a representative of the Commissioner of Police.

When the undertaker went to his shed to get the shell, which was needed for another body, he found he could not lift it. He procured a light and called the workmen. Both were terrified, one crying out that the body was 'the ghost of Constable Parker.'

The most remarkable thing is that, when lifting it, neither of the men noticed the weight of the coffin, although the dead man weighed 15 st. Each thought the other must be shouldering the greater part of the weight.

Daily Mail, 1922

The Man who Complained about His Funeral

A funeral service held for August Simolke in Chicago is causing him a lot of worry. Simolke, 67, says the wrong man was buried, and he does not see why his family should pay the funeral bills.

Three months after Simolke disappeared, leaving a wife and eleven children, a man answering his description was found dead in an hotel.

Just after Mrs Simolke had paid for the 965-dollar funeral, a Christmas card arrived from her husband who was working in a lumber camp.

Mr Simolke is protesting because he does not like the idea of anyone else in his grave.

Grit, 1949

A Dry Run

Timothy Dexter, a queer character from Massachusetts, USA, arranged his own funeral rehearsal, and afterwards at home beat his wife because she had not shed enough tears at his graveside.

Reveille, 1959

Transports of Delight

Things that go Bump in the Street

Shoppers gasped as a hearse drove solemnly past a bustling market. For suddenly out slid the coffin.

The hearse's back door had swung open as it turned an uphill corner. And as the coffin hit the road, the lid fell off, revealing the corpse.

A passer-by dragged the coffin to the roadside.

Five minutes later the hearse driver glanced over his shoulder . . . and did a screeching U-turn. Horrified, he raced back to Broadway Market in London's East End.

He and his assistant were relieved to find the coffin was undamaged and, after loading it back in the hearse, drove off.

Daily Star, 1982

The Last Lap

The last wish of Walter St John Brice, aged 73, of Hoo, near Rochester, was that he should be buried as he had lived – at speed.

In his will he desired that on his last journey the hearse ('not a Ford') should be 'driven at speed, because I always hated loitering.'

His daughter-in-law said: 'He used to get into his car and shoot off. His motto was: "Get on with the job".'

Sunday Express, 1949

26

Eternal Recurrence

A curious coincidence is reported from the village of
Quarnford, near Buxton. A motor hearse containing the
body of Mrs Bruce Palmer overturned in exactly the same
spot as the taxicab containing Mr and Mrs Palmer returning
from the church overturned after their wedding.

Mr J. Newton, a Buxton baker, was delivering bread near
the spot on both occasions, and helped to right the vehicles.

Daily News, 1925

The Late Show

Sam R. Kimball, an aged Californian rancher, has placed an
order for a £240 steel coffin equipped with a wireless
receiving set.

Kimball explained that he is convinced the soul lingers
near the body until the Day of Judgment, and that he will be
able to 'hear what is going on in the world'.

Weekly Dispatch, 1925

May the Force be with You

A hearse containing a coffin had only moved a short distance
from a house in Bath when it suddenly overturned.

'I have never seen anything like it,' the driver said. 'The
hearse seemed to be lifted up bodily and thrown forward. It
was on a perfectly flat surface, and there was no skidding.'

Daily Express, 1924

Never Say Die

Phobias of premature burial

I Want to Live!

Mrs Chrissie Fraser turned up alive at her sister's home in
Aberdeen ten days after the coroner recorded a verdict that
she died in a Paddington Hotel bathroom.

But the coroner refused to alter his verdict and said she
must apply to the High Court if she wanted to be brought
back to life.

'It's awful to feel that I am supposed to be dead,' said Mrs
Fraser. 'It doesn't feel very nice. The worry of it has made me
ill. I don't want to go on being dead.'

Daily Mail, 1961

A Hell of an Experience

A group of Buddhist monks were chanting funeral rites
around the coffin of 91-year-old nun Lee Che in Hong Kong.

The coffin lid was open and the still figure of Lee Che was
dressed in a shroud. Suddenly the corpse sat up and asked
for a cup of tea. Pandemonium broke loose and the monks
fled.

When order was finally restored Lee Che explained: 'I
have been to the gates of hell escorted by two guards – one
with the head of an ox, the other with the face of a horse.

'But at the gates they sent me back. I suppose I was a bit
early.'

Weekend, 1964

Mrs Cowling's Off-Day

The news that 80-year-old Mrs Emily Cowling had died was a shock to many people in Yorkshire.

Mrs Cowling had worked hard for sick and old folk, and a meeting of old people stood for two minutes in silent remembrance of her.

Wreaths were sent to Mrs Cowling's home. There to receive them was a surprised Mrs Cowling.

She said: 'I only stayed home for a few days because I felt ill.'

The next day she married 90-year-old Joseph Robinson and left for a honeymoon in Blackpool.

Reveille, 1954

Dead Man's Handle

An application has been lodged with the US Patent Office from a man who wants to make sure he is not buried alive.

The device consists of a chimney which protrudes from the casket, and a lever within easy reach of the dead. When life is restored the 'dead' squeeze a handle wired up to the chimney to: (1) Ring a bell in the house of the cemetery sexton; (2) Cause an arm mounted on the chimney to wave up and down above ground to attract attention; (3) Supply the casket with oxygen until the grave is opened.

Toronto Star Weekly, 1948

Ring for Attention

At a recent London inquest the coroner was asked whether it would be advisable in some cases of sudden death to put bells on the hands and feet of the corpse in case of life not really being quite extinct.

Daily Telegraph, 1922

"It's to commemorate the unknown deserter".

We Shall Remember Them

Monsieur Jacques Roumieu has asked that his name be removed from the local war memorial at Carcassonne, South of France.

Sunday Express, 1954

Oops!

The following letter appeared in an American newspaper recently: 'Sir–I desire to call your attention to a few errors in your obituary notice of myself on Wednesday last.

'I was born in Washington, not Wheeler, and my retirement from the flour and feed business was not due to ill health, but hard times. The cause of my death was not pneumonia.'

World's Press News, 1930

A Pretty Needling Experience

We had a new ship's doctor on our voyage to Australia.

A few days out of port a fireman dropped dead from a heart attack in his surgery. I ordered the body to be taken to the fo'castle and sewn in canvas while the funeral was arranged.

In the quiet of the fo'castle where the bosun was performing his gruesome task, there was a sudden dreadful shriek.

Unwrapping the canvas, I saw the corpse was breathing and had blood on its nose. The doctor was summoned and he ordered the man to the sick bay.

I asked the bosun what caused the fearful yell.

'I must have stuck this needle through Fireman Atkinson's nose as I sewed him up,' he said.

Later Fireman Atkinson asked me what the two holes were in his nose for.

'The doctor made them to help you to breathe better when you were ill,' I lied.

I asked the doctor how the man had died. He confessed that it was not a heart attack. He had given Fireman Atkinson a cup of carbolic in mistake for medicine.

'That was pretty careless of you,' I said.

In reply the doctor handed me his resignation.

Reveille, 1963

Right Grave–Wrong Body

The relatives stood round the graveside as they lowered the coffin containing Roberto Rodriguez, who had 'died' of a heart attack.

The lid of the coffin suddenly burst open, and Roberto sat up, shouting to the amazed mourners that he was still alive.

It happened in Venezuela. Roberto was saved–but the shock killed his mother-in-law, who was later buried in the same grave.

Weekend, 1962

Sorry–the Line's Gone Dead

A Blackburn woman, Mrs Eliza Bankes, who now lives in Birmingham, USA, has no fear of death–but she does not want to be buried alive, so she has made arrangements for her tomb to be on the phone.

A specially designed coffin has air holes and is fitted with the latest type of microphone telephone, placed in such a position that, even if she were buried alive, Mrs Bankes could still ring up the local exchange and tell them so.

Everybody's Weekly, 1937

Fresh to the Last Drop

A moment before the mourners at a funeral in the Thaton district of South Burma would have lowered the coffin into its grave, a muffled voice was heard.

Hastily the lid was opened.

'Give me a drink!' the 'dead' man gasped.

They gave him some water. Then, with a cry of horror, he jumped out of the coffin and rushed home in his shroud.

Daily Mail, 1934

Dead Beat

The front tyre of a hearse punctured on a broken bottle near a Mexico cemetery, and the hearse struck a tree and killed the driver.

Then mourners heard thuds from the coffin and muffled cries of 'I'm not dead,' and 'Don't bury me.'

The 'corpse', Teodomira Marin Zarate, 43, of Elefino, near Toluca, who had apparently dropped dead after a hard day's work, is now described as 'alive and well'.

Daily Mail, 1947

All Wrapped Up and Nowhere To Go

A strange funeral took place at Harpurhey Cemetery, Manchester. It was that of Miss Beswick, of Hollinwood House, who died about 100 years before her burial.

She had a horror of being buried alive, and by her will she left most of her property to her physician, on condition that he undertook to keep her above ground as long as possible.

Quite agreeable to this condition, the doctor mummified the body by coating it with tar and wrapping it in bandages. In this state it figured for many years as an exhibit in the Manchester Natural History Museum.

Manchester Guardian, 1938

Buried in a Butty Box

Christian Straube occupies a small hut in the woods of Richland, New Jersey. His furniture consists of a stove, a small table, a cot, a chair–and a coffin.

The owner's pride in the coffin is because of its completeness.

In the cover, above the place where the man's nose will be, is a hole in which a ten foot pipe will extend to the surface for fresh air. On top of the pipe is a large bell connected to a rope placed in the occupant's hand so that he can ring for rescue.

Straube, who does not believe in embalming, has since his youth feared the possibility of being buried alive.

A fresh sandwich is made every two or three days, the last one to be placed in his hand immediately after death.

Weekly Telegraph, 1920

Third Time Lucky

Twice Johan Kovacs, of Montenegro, Yugoslavia, was
pronounced dead.

On the first occasion he was found to be breathing while
on the undertaker's slab.

When he opened his eyes he nearly had a heart attack at
the sight of the coffin. Doctors said he had been in a trance.

Then he 'died' a second time. His wife was in no hurry to
call the undertaker this time. One week later Johan sat up in
bed and asked for a drink.

Weekend, 1982

Dead Drunk

The student lowered his knife carefully, pierced the skin of
the body laid out on the dissection-room table–and there
was a loud cry: 'Oh, that hurts!'

The 'body' sprang off the table and made for the door and
the student collapsed.

This was the remarkable sequel to the supposed death of
Jose Ines Anguinaino, who had been found on the outskirts
of Celaya, near Mexico City, suffering from a bad attack of
alcoholic poisoning.

For seventy-two hours he had lain in the hospital morgue,
whence he had then been removed to the dissection room for
a post-mortem.

The touch of the knife revived him. He is now recovering,
sitting up and eating with evident relish.

The student is in bed suffering from severe shock.

Portsmouth Evening News, 1938

Last Laughs

Make 'em Laugh . . .

The proceedings of the Royal Society record the case of John Davis, of Birmingham, who in the year 1862 gave a piece of tobacco enclosed in bread to an elephant. He laughed so heartily at the animal's displeasure that he fell dead from heart failure.

Halfpenny Short Cuts, 1891

A Roman named Crassus was sitting by the roadside when he saw an ass choked by a thistle, and was so convulsed with laughter that he ruptured a blood vessel and died on the spot.

Golden Penny, 1895

Mr Joseph Chatfield, a 79-year-old retired builder, of Lonsdale Road, Barnes, collapsed and died from excessive laughter while watching a Charlie Chaplin film in a Hammersmith cinema.

His housekeeper said: 'I do not think I have ever seen him laugh so much before. He suddenly passed away in my arms.'

Daily Mirror, 1923

A Funny Thing Happened on the Way to the Cemetery . . .

Charles Lundy, ex-funeral attendant and crematorium assistant, has launched himself on a career as Britain's most unlikely after-dinner speaker.

He's hoping to rock 'em in the aisles with rollicking tales of graveside gaffes and cemetery slip-ups.

Like . . . 'A funny thing happened to the short-sighted hearse driver on the way to the cemetery. He missed his turning and wound up in a cellar, coffin and all.'

And the one about the widow moved to tears when her late husband's former workmates gathered outside the factory as the cortege passed by.

What she didn't know was that they were all out on strike picket duty.

Or the time Chas, of Glazebrook, Warrington, went to the wrong house to lay out a corpse.

'I've come to take your grandad to Heaven,' he explained to a curious youngster at the door.

'Well, you'll have to wait,' said the little lad. 'He's just popped down to Tesco's with my Mam.'

Daily Mirror, 1983

In Laughing Memory

Amateur actor Philip Cronan had them in stitches on the stage . . . even after his death.

For when the old trooper finally bowed out, his family put an obituary notice in the local paper, written in the humorous style they knew 80-year-old Philip would have loved.

It read: 'Following my rapid departure, I am now pleased to announce that plans are under way for my next production.

'Facilities here are good, the stage is somewhat bigger and casting should be a lot easier. Those wishing to attend auditions should contact me—in your own time.'

Daily Star, 1983

Save the Last Dance for Me

A man named Baldwin left directions for a slab to be placed over his grave in Lymington, Hampshire, but his wife declared that she would dance on it.

To thwart her, Baldwin altered his will and left instructions that his body would be buried at sea, off the Needles.

Titbits, 1945

By Eck!

Earl Peel, who lives in Richmond, has been telling the story of the tombstone that a Yorkshireman had ordered for his late wife, to include the words 'She Was Thine.'

When he went to see the finished work, he was horrified to see that it read: 'She Was Thin.'

He complained to the engraver: 'You've left out the ''e'',' and a correction was promised.

On his second visit the inscription read: 'E! She Was Thin.'

Daily Telegraph, 1982

Gone but not Forgotten

Stumped

Crisco the magician was left a baffling bequest in a stranger's will . . . the dead man's body complete with artificial leg. And even Crisco's magic powers were not enough to solve the riddle of what to do with the corpse.

He conjured up a brainwave, and offered the body for medical research.

But doctors turned it down because it only had one leg.

Bemused Crisco–real name Christopher Cox of Ryde, Isle of Wight–thinks the eerie episode was a macabre joke by someone who saw his magic act years ago.

'Apparently he'd met me briefly thirteen years ago after seeing my comedy magic act. I never saw him again.

'The only things he left behind were an artificial leg, a wheelchair and a book on black magic.'

Crisco could not trace any of the dead man's family as he had three different aliases. He decided to give the mystery body a decent funeral and invited forty of his own friends.

News of the World, 1983

Eternal Rest

It was a very grave matter when Monsieur Paul Gerard passed away. But someone had a notice put in a Paris newspaper which said: 'During his hard-working life, he was married six times. Death mercifully relieved him of his sufferings.'

Weekend, 1965

The Finger of Suspicion

Boston police were puzzled by a series of successful bank raids around the city.

The only clue found in each case was a single thumb-print on the safe. It was finally identified as that of gangster Ben Franklin who had been murdered some time previously.

Detectives, acting on a tip, hid inside a bank and watched the raiders at work. They filled several suitcases with banknotes and jewelry.

Then, before making their escape, one of them slipped a human thumb out of his pocket and pressed it on the safe handle.

After being arrested they confessed that the ploy had earned them a total of £250,000.

Answers, 1940

The One that Got Away

When a keen angler died last year in Louisiana, USA, his coffin was placed in a grave hewn from the rocks in the middle of a shallow river thirty miles from his home.

On his deathbed he had expressed a wish to lie in the river at the exact spot where, fifty years earlier, his father had given him his first fishing lesson.

He also directed that angling friends attending the funeral should bring their tackle with them and hold a fishing competition immediately after the burial. The winner was to receive a prize of £166.

Reveille, 1954

Dead Ignorant

Some years ago football coupons were being sent to Mr William Wilberforce – at the address he occupied when he was advocating the abolition of slavery some 160 years ago.

Reveille, 1962

The Last Supper

An odd deathbed request was recently made by a New York banker.

An hour before he died he asked that three of his best friends be invited to dinner on the evening before his funeral.

The meal was to be served on the lid of the coffin after it had been screwed down, and was to consist of soup, chicken, trifle and coffee.

'It will be our last meal together,' said the banker.

Titbits, 1950

. . . And the Last Post

Subscribers in California, for a minimum of £20, can send 'heavengrams' to their dear departed ones.

The service is run by Gabe Gabor who collects the loving messages on a special form before handing them to a terminally ill 'courier' for passing on in the afterlife.

There is also a priority service where a message is placed with three couriers, 'increasing the chance of early delivery.'

Titbits, 1982

"I'm afraid she wants this one sent express."

Wrestling the Grim Reaper

A Pathetique Excuse

Victor Kolar, the conductor, has flatly refused to direct Tchaikovsky's Sixth Symphony for dancer Olga Fricker.

'There is not enough money in the world to make me play the Pathetique again,' he said.

Costumes had been ordered and the choreography completed, but Kolar was adamant.

'In the last twenty-five years I have played the movement fifteen times, and after each performance someone has died.'

Everybody's Weekly, 1938

The Last Trip Home

Soldier Danvers died after an unfortunate accident. After serving with a Yorkshire regiment in the Second World War, he escaped death on the Dunkirk beaches, and was among the last to be evacuated from Singapore.

He survived his ship being sunk in the Indian Ocean, then went through the Burma campaign.

On returning to England he went on leave to his home town, Sheffield. On the second day he tripped over the front doorstep, broke his neck and died instantly.

Weekend, 1981

The Most Unpopular Popular Song

A strange trail of death is linked with the song 'Gloomy Sunday' which claimed at least twenty-five suicides before being banned by the BBC.

It was written by Hungarian composer Reszo Seress whose girlfriend had jilted him for a rich man. When it was published and became popular she committed suicide.

When it was played by a gipsy orchestra in Budapest a government official shot himself after writing down the words; a girl of 14 poisoned herself and left a note saying the song had affected her; a woman bought a record of the tune and killed herself.

The publishers withdrew the song, but it was recorded in the USA and soon five people took their lives after listening to it.

Everybody's Weekly, 1936

Tripping the Light Fantastic

A young, very stout and tall American lady was engaged to a short, slim man. On the eve of the wedding he called to see her, and as, overjoyed, she rushed downstairs to meet him, she tripped, fell on top of him and broke his neck.

Daily Express, 1927

Oh Elk!

Three sportsmen went out to shoot elks in Norway when a mountain mist overtook and separated them. One unfortunate man, approaching another of the party, looked so enormous in the fog that his companion mistook him for an elk and shot him dead.

Spectator, 1928

All Strung Up

Mrs Alice Cullimore, of Birmingham, ate supper and went out to meet her husband. Soon afterwards she called upon a neighbour, evidently suffering great pain, and pleaded that her corsets should be cut.

This was done, but the woman died. A verdict of natural causes, hastened by tight lacing, was returned.

Daily Chronicle, 1926

Disgusted, Italy

Italian Antonio Vajente fell in love with a Frenchwoman fifty years ago, but she chose another man.

Recently they met again and, though still free, she would not marry him. Antonio threw himself under a train at Vincenza.

The driver managed to stop in time–so the 73-year-old bachelor went into a field and stabbed himself.

Daily Mail, 1949

Delayed Action

When Texan Henry Ziegland jilted his country sweetheart to marry a rich widow, the girl's brother tried to kill him.

He followed Henry into the woods, and shot at him with his revolver. Ziegland threw himself to the ground, and the brother, thinking he had killed him, then turned the gun on himself. The bullet, in fact, had missed and lodged in a tree.

Years later Henry visited a wood he had bought to supervise workmen dynamiting the trees to clear the ground. He watched the men bore a hole in a tree–unaware that it was the same one in which the bullet intended for him had lodged.

The dynamite was fired and Ziegland fell to the ground dead. The explosion had driven out the bullet, which killed him outright.

Guide and Ideas, 1938

Hot-Shot

In October 1936 a Hungarian colonel was bereaved by a kiss.
As he embraced his wife his loaded revolver went off
accidentally and killed her.

Reveille, 1938

Taken to Heart

Edward Hill, a Texas farmer, spent three weeks in a Dallas
hospital for a minor heart condition. He soon recovered, but
on the way out he was handed a bill for his medical
treatment.

He took one horrified look, collapsed and died of shock.
The bill for the three weeks was £27,000.

Titbits, 1982

"And then there's the mortuary bill ...."

Some Things Never Change

The Courts of Justice in Paris received a letter from a Marseilles judge, stating that Emile Jacquard should not be executed.

Jacquard had been found guilty of murder and sentenced to death. But on receiving unquestionable evidence of the condemned man's innocence, the local judge wrote hastily to Paris.

By the time the letter arrived the unfortunate man had been guillotined. This was not, perhaps, surprising. The letter had been posted in 1902 and reached Paris thirty-six years later.

Weekend, 1982

The Big Kiss-Off of 1905

Donald St John, an assistant in an Australian grocers, kissed a customer, Miss Lillie Isabel Dickson, in 1905 'because it was a beautiful Spring morning'.

He was fined £2, plus 50p costs and bound over to keep the peace for six months. Ten years later Miss Dickson died and left him £20,000 'for the pleasure derived from the only kiss I ever had from a man'.

Reveille, 1930

Fallen Hero

World War I hero Major Francis S. Moller MC, DFC, RFC, had more wound-stripes than any other British soldier.

The war exploits of the 'Mad Major', in tanks and in the trenches, were legendary. He is said to have tackled enemy squadrons single-handed.

After the war he retired to the Seychelle Islands where he died when his verandah collapsed.

Leader Magazine, 1949

Palmed Off

When Carlos Castro was told by a fortune-teller that he was about to die, he spent his life savings buying a coffin and treating everyone in his home village of Trapani, Sicily, to a farewell drink. The bill came to £450.

But on the day forecast for his death nothing happened. Now Carlos plans to sue the fortune-teller.

Titbits, 1983

Stone Me!

Sir,

Just over a year ago our son attended his grandmother's funeral. While he was paying his last respects a gravestone toppled over onto his leg.

It took two men to lift off, it was so heavy. His new suit was ruined.

Our son could have been killed. This time it is the price of a new suit. Perhaps another person won't be so lucky . . .

South Wales Echo, 1982

Upstaged

While Mr C. J. Stone, a local undertaker, was conducting the funeral of a friend at Melcombe Regis cemetery, Weymouth, today, he suddenly pitched forward over the open grave. When he was picked up he was dead.

There were 200 people present and many women screamed. The mourners were led away, the service being continued afterwards.

Mrs Stone, the widow, learned the news of her husband's death from a newspaper contents bill.

Daily Express, 1925

Cash in the Vaults

A charity fund has cut its links with a fund-raiser—because of his morbid obsession with death.

Robert Cummings claims he has slept next to a corpse inside a coffin at a mortuary.

And he raised £35 by spending the night at a haunted castle where 100 years ago a man killed himself after committing a murder.

A charity trust director wrote to him saying: 'I am rather disturbed by your fascination with death. We cannot allow you to collect money for us in this way.'

Ex-lorry driver Robert, of Moreton, Merseyside, said: 'I can't deny it. I often attend funerals as a social outing.'

The Sun, 1982

The World's most Unsuccessful Artist

Hans Kinnow, a Budapest painter, flung the last splash of colour on his canvas and looked back at his model with a smile.

Within a few hours her millionaire husband would be signing a cheque for the completed work.

Suddenly the model, with a cry of pain, slipped to the ground, dead from heart failure.

His next sitter, a wealthy banker, was so pleased with his portrait that he added a bonus to the fee. As his servants were adjusting the picture on the walls of his mansion, the banker took ill. Two days later he was dead.

Kinnow shrugged it off as a coincidence. Then the third sitter, the daughter of a Budapest actor, died a few days after he had set down his brush.

The artist abandoned his fourth portrait and vowed never to paint again.

A year later he decided to marry. His bride-to-be asked Kinnow to paint her picture as a wedding present.

Kinnow pleaded tiredness, but his fiancé insisted. He painted the portrait, watching her anxiously.

The sitting passed without incident. Then, a week later, she caught pneumonia and expired.

Kinnow gave up painting and earned his living as a messenger. In April 1938 police found him dead in a lodging house.

Among his belongings was a self-portrait, dated the previous day.

Weekly Telegraph, 1949

The Lions' Share

A religious fanatic attempted to recreate the story of Daniel in the lions' den in Perth, Western Australia.

The man, in his 40s, wearing several crucifixes and medallions, got out of his car in a safari park and walked to where some lions were feeding. Sixteen of them jumped on him and ate him.

Daily Mirror, 1982

Death is Sweet . . .

A freak shot from a rifle discharged in a workshop killed a man in Melbourne.

When the trigger caught on a workman's coat the bullet passed through a paling fence, a birdcage–missing the love-bird inside–the weatherboard of a house, and a wooden dresser, before striking 33-year-old George Horner in the chest.

It would have missed him, too, but for his bad luck in standing up to get sugar for his tea.

The Star, 1945

No Bones About It

What they did with the left-overs

Psst!

They prowl the grounds of Harare Hospital in Zimbabwe with sympathetic-looking faces. Their eyes ready to shed crocodile tears.

Small-time undertakers have suddenly mushroomed all over the city. Every morning their first stop is the hospital mortuary where they greet the attendants with the customary: 'How many dead today?'

The Harare Hospital administrator, Mrs Margaret Chidzonga, was on one occasion approached by a man in the hospital grounds and offered a coffin 'on easy terms.'

'Sometimes they walk into the wards during visiting time looking for seriously ill patients. Then they offer funeral services before the person is even dead,' said Mrs Chidzonga.

If someone comes with a car and a coffin to claim the body of a dead relative, the small-time undertakers deflate the car tyres, then offer their own transport at more than three times the normal cost.

Harare Herald, 1983

The Iron Man

One of the strangest fates that ever befell was that of a man who fell into a melting-pot of molten steel at Woolwich. Of course he vanished utterly and instantly.

His body, reduced to imperceptible atoms, was disseminated through the mass of the molten metal.

The War Office authorities decided that this could not be properly used for warlike purposes, and so it was run into an ingot and this was buried in accordance with the rites of the Church of England.

Pearson's Weekly, 1896

Dem Bones, Dem Bones

If clarinet music sounds sweeter in Bologna, Italy, this year musicians should thank one of their colleagues who died a few months ago.

He drew up a will which would allow him to take part in the musical life of the city—even after his death. Instructions were recently carried out to make his bones into clarinet mouthpieces.

Reveille, 1952

Laugh? I Nearly Died

An inhabitant of Montgaillard recently left the following testament: 'It is my will that any one of my relations who shall presume to shed tears at my funeral shall be disinherited. The sole heir will be he who laughs most heartily.'

Chamber's Edinburgh Journal, 1837

An Old Timer

Grandad Tom Gribble knows what he wants to happen when he dies. He wants to come back as an egg-timer.

And he's put it in his will to make it official.

He says his ashes must be used to replace the sand in a timer.

'I hope the timer will be handed down from generation to generation and the owner will be able to say, "That's my great-great-grandpa",' said 62-year-old Tom of Henbury, Bristol.

He hoped that one of his two daughters could use him to time the family's boiled eggs.

'Because of my bad legs I can't work, but one day I'll be of some use again.'

Daily Mirror, 1983

"He always was a rotten timekeeper."

All at Sea

Sailor Len Johnson's relatives were delivered a stunning
blow when he died. His ashes got lost in the post.

When Len died in Holland undertakers mailed his urn to
Britain for his ashes to be scattered at sea.

But ten days later they had still not arrived. Frantic
relatives contacted the Prime Minister and all sorting offices
were alerted.

The urn was eventually found in Mount Pleasant post
office, London.

Daily Mirror, 1983

Alas Poor Andre

In a bizarre bequest London-based pianist Andrew
Tchaikowski has left his head to the Royal Shakespeare
Company.

Tchaikowski nursed a peculiar hankering to become an
actor during his life. He died with that ambition unfulfilled.

But his moment came when he willed his head to the RSC
to be used as a skull in the famous graveyard scene in
Hamlet.

The company's artistic director Terry Hands surprised
Oxford undertakers Reeves and Pain by accepting the
bequest. An operation was completed which will allow the
RSC to use Mr Tchaikowski's remains in their next
production.

But the unique bequest may yet fail to be cast for the job—
some actors are none too keen to spend half the performance
stuck down a hole in the stage with human remains.

Some actors prefer a plastic skull. The real thing tends to
break easily.

Daily Express, 1982

All Human Life is There

At the paperworks where this magazine is printed there is a huge vat of boiling pulp in which cruelly-toothed wheels revolve, mashing the fragments into minute uniformity.

A few days ago the man whose duty it was to feed this vat disappeared. He had been seen one minute and the next he was gone.

By next morning the terrible conclusion became inevitable that he had slipped on some bit of greasy waste and fallen over the edge of the vat.

Meanwhile the great rolls of paper from that particular vatful of pulp had been devoured by the presses at the rate of 20,000 copies of *Pearson's Weekly* to the hour. By the time news reached this office recall was impossible.

It is gruesome to the point of fascination. The stream of thought passing from the printed page might be set in motion by words printed on a page into which were incorporated the eyes and brain of this unhappy man.

The paper held by living hands might actually be partly made of the flesh and bones and sinews of his. His body, subdivided into an infinity of particles, has been scattered far and wide, not only over the United Kingdom, but over half the seas and lands of the civilized world.

Pearson's Weekly, 1890

Jacques-Pot

A Frenchman unwittingly took a lottery ticket to his grave. He had put the ticket in the pocket of his suit and was later buried in it.

When the result of the lottery was announced his widow realized the missing ticket entitled her to about £1000.

She persuaded the coroner to allow his body to be exhumed, found the ticket—and claimed the money.

Reveille, 1963

Resurrection Shuttle

Time traveller Sid Hills is taking bookings for a one-way ticket to Eternity.

So far he has had forty inquiries about a charter flight to sunny California – for corpses. The resurrection shuttle will whisk clients on a bizarre package trip to have their bodies frozen in time capsules.

And if they can't afford to travel full-fare there are reductions – hard up customers can simply have their head sent instead.

Lancashire Evening Post, 1980

A Thumping Good Idea

An American who died recently left funds for converting his own skin into a drum. He bequeathed £1000 to a naturalist friend, on condition that he prepared the skin and chose two suitable bones for drumsticks so the drum could be beaten at sunrise every July 17th at the foot of Bunker Hill.

Reveille, 1950

There's no Arm in It

Frank Ives, the American billiard champion, can strike a ball
with a cue harder than any man in the world. One quick,
sharp blow and the ball flies round the table striking eleven
cushions.

Men striking it with all the force they possess cannot come
within a dozen feet of his record. Eminent physicians can
give no explanation for Ives' skill, except to say that his
profession has led to the development of muscles even prize
fighters do not use.

To enlighten others after his death Ives has now left orders
in his will that his right arm be severed from his body and
sent to his physician so that the secret might be discovered.
The rest of him he desires to be cremated.

Pearson's Weekly, 1896

Hornswaggled

Canada. Calgary cattleman Jake Fitte mounts the heads of
his favourite bulls on a cattleshed wall when they die, but a
court has refused him permission to do the same with the
head of his late wife Yvonne, killed in a car crash.

Titbits, 1981

A Clean Sweep

Oil lamp manufacturer Sydney Sherwood left £160,384, and
directions that his ashes be scattered on the floor of his
Birmingham factory 'because of his affection for the works',
said his secretary—just before the ashes were neatly swept
up again. It had always been an orderly factory.

Daily Mail, 1983

Last Orders

This Round is on Me . . .

Each night at sunset a woman with a bottle of wine attends to the grave of her husband in the cemetery of a small Californian town.

She pours the wine into a glass and, with a prayer, empties it over the head of the grave. Then silently she puts the bottle and glass back into her handbag and walks away.

The woman has been performing the strange ceremony daily for five years to comply with her husband's will.

It stated: 'While my cellar shall last it shall be used for my purpose only. Each evening at sunset a glass of the finest wine shall be emptied over my body. If any of the wine touches the lips of my family before my cellar is empty, they will lose their inheritance.'

Everybody's Weekly, 1937

The Greater Plan

When Mr Saynor, a 67-year-old war veteran from Yorkshire, died, his last wish was to be buried in his back garden.

Mr Saynor, who had been a professional wrestler in his time, and was known as the 'Manacled Madman', also wished to have a piper play the lament *Flowers of the Forest*, a bugler to sound the *Reveille* and *Last Post* and a contingent from his old regiment to fire a salute.

Leeds City Council Environmental Health Department refused planning permission for the garden burial. One of the aspects authorities have to bear in mind is whether the grave would have a detrimental effect on the re-sale value of the house in future years.

Funeral Director, 1982

Earthly Comforts

Strange requests for his funeral arrangements have been made by the Rev. Addison J. Wheeler, vicar of Thursley, near Godalming, in a letter to parishioners which has aroused much comment in that part of Surrey.

After declaring that all our death customs are an abomination, he asks: 'For my coffin, just an open box, made by anyone with a saw and hammer and nails in half an hour. As there will be plenty of room I would like a few of my bedside books and my hot-water bottle.'

Daily Chronicle, 1930

The Drive-in Funeral

Police battled to control jostling spectators and TV cameramen as fun-loving Sandra West sat at the wheel of her blue sports car wearing just a baby-doll nightie.

But Sandra, a 37-year-old heiress from San Antonio, was unable to enjoy the occasion—because the event was her own funeral.

Her dying wish had been 'to be buried next to my husband, in my lace nightgown, and sitting in the sports car he gave me'.

Just before the burial the authorities insisted that the car was placed in a wooden crate, and two truck loads of cement were poured into the grave to discourage vandals.

Weekend, 1983

Pie in the Sky Legacy

Mr and Mrs Richard Selly of Houston, the spaceshot city in Texas, thought it was their lucky day when a long-forgotten cousin left them a million dollars.

But there was one very tall order . . . the will required them to bury their cousin on the moon.

Weekend, 1982

The Final Service

Mattoon, Ill. (AP) Mechanic Harvey Wishart, 68, was buried with one of his favourite automobiles on Friday.

Wishart had tinkered with engines most of his life and, in accordance with his request, a 200 lb automobile was lowered into his grave.

The car had only one seat.

Daily Express, 1948

Granny's Song of Farewell

The dying wish of great-grandmother Ethel Gilliard was granted yesterday when mourners following her coffin sang the Gracie Fields classic *Wish Me Luck As You Wave Me Goodbye*.

The fifty relatives and friends were accompanied through the streets of Nailsworth, Gloucestershire, by the village band.

Mrs Gilliard, 90, had supported the band for sixty-three years.

Bandmaster Bill Bruton said: 'She told me this was what she wanted. It was the finest tribute we could pay her.'

Daily Mirror, 1983

In Loving Memory

Monumental reminders

Move Over . . .

A woman in Cookville, Tennessee, who was twice widowed, has reserved space for herself between the graves of her two husbands. She has already installed her own tombstone which says simply: 'Their wife'.

Reveille, 1954

The Last Toast

In the little churchyard of Brightling, Sussex, is a huge pyramid which is the tomb of John Fuller, a wealthy but eccentric bachelor who built it twenty-four years before his death.

The former MP for Rose Hill left orders for his body to be placed inside, sitting upright in an armchair with a bottle of claret in one hand and a glass of wine in the other.

Home Words, 1932

Nice One, Roy

A 54-year-old postman who lighted up his wife's casket with a neon sign, held open house last night in the red brick mausoleum he outfitted as a living room.

Roy Acklin, of St Petersburg, Florida, was host to several hundred persons who dropped by for a look or a chat.

The 15 sq ft tomb is furnished with an electric fan, ashtrays, chair, wall ornaments, potted plants and a guest book.

Back of the casket a blue neon sign spells out his wife's name—Beulah. In the corners, fluorescent red and yellow lights burn at night.

The light bill runs to about six dollars a month, Acklin explained.

Associated Press, 1949

Welcome Home Darling

A tombstone with the bride's name inscribed on it was presented by a bridegroom to his wife when they returned to Chicago from their honeymoon.

Giving evidence in subsequent divorce proceedings, the bride said that her husband took her to his garage and showed her the tombstone as soon as they arrived home.

Titbits, 1945

Food for Thought

Baker Pete McGee, of Mearnskirk, near Glasgow, had a stone oven in need of repair, but he was short of money. So one night he climbed into a nearby graveyard, collected some discarded gravestones, and built them into a new oven.

His customers got a shock next day. The batch of loaves came out stamped in reverse 'Sacred to the Memory of . . .'

Weekend, 1980

Fourth Time Lucky

When Canon M. Gadenne, parish priest of Roches, France, reached the age of 74 he was sure he would not live much longer.

He ordered a stone bearing the inscription: 'M. Gadenne, died 188–.' The last figure was omitted, for carving later.

In 1890 he was still alive and, as the old tombstone was out of date, bought a new one bearing the incomplete date '189–.'

Ten years later he was still alive, but being sure he was approaching the end of his life, he ordered a third dated '190–.' But even that was not used.

In 1911, at the age of 105, he ordered another inscribed 'M. Gadenne, died 19––.' He died soon afterwards.

Reveille, 1961

Roll Out the Barrel

A grave in Heidelberg Cemetery, near Melbourne, Australia, has beer barrels carved in marble. It belongs to a woman who was addicted to drink but managed to conquer the habit.

Reveille, 1950

A Lotta Bottle

Farmer John Waring doesn't have fairies at the bottom of his garden–just Eva, a most remarkable lady.

She was buried there after a funeral service conducted by her owner, Mr Waring, of Pocklington, Humberside, who explains: 'Eva was a very special dairy cow.'

In nineteen years she provided milk for 300,000 doorsteps. Eva lies next to her mother, 'a tremendous cow', in graves dug by a mechanical digger which will soon have headstones and beds of flowers.

Mr Waring continues to mourn Eva. He says: 'She was like Red Rum. This is the end of the greatest cow.'

Weekend, 1983

A Monumental Affair

Retired Mid-Western farmer John Davis, an 82-year-old widower, has lavished millions of dollars on his own love story in marble.

He started the memorial following his wife's death. It now consists of eleven magnificent life-sized models sculptured in Italy, showing Farmer Davis and his wife in various stages of courtship and marriage.

Everybody is charmed with the idea except his in-laws, who see his devotion to his wife's memory as a baser plan to deprive them of his wealth.

Sunday Pictorial, 1937

FIRST ARGUMENT

Headache Tablet

British Rail is sitting on what looks like a world record. The organization has managed to lose a hefty stone tablet, a full 2 ft square, for the past thirty-five years.

It's a memorial to Rowland Ding the pioneer World War I pilot who died on a 1917 test flight.

Chums at a Leeds aeronautics factory put up the tablet in his honour, but the factory closed down in 1946. The family asked for the stone to be sent to Ding's old school in Kent— and that was the last anybody saw of it.

The family thought it had arrived safely, but now Ding's daughter Aphra Burley has found it disappeared somewhere between Leeds and Canterbury.

She says: 'I'm not frightfully optimistic, but the thing is 2 ft square and not easy to lose.'

Daily Express, 1983

In Passing . . .

Stanley Moore was about to be married when he was overcome with stomach-ache.

The pains were so bad that he was unable to go through with the wedding. Later, he discovered that a jealous rival had slipped a large dose of laxative into his coffee on the morning of the wedding.

The ceremony never took place and Mr Moore remained a bachelor.

When he died in Philadelphia thirty years later he left all his money, a small fortune, to the firm that manufactured the laxative.

Reveille, 1960